Spiritual Rea...

For Funerals and Mem...

Compiled by Hugh Morrison

Montpelier Publishing
London
MMXIV

ISBN-13: 978-1503379329
Published by Montpelier Publishing, London.
Printed by Amazon Createspace.
Set in Calibri 11pt.
This edition copyright © 2014. All rights reserved.

Sunlit radiance

Who does not remember the story of the Christian missionary in Britain, sitting one evening in the vast hall of a Saxon king, surrounded by his thanes, having come thither to preach the gospel of his Master; and as he spoke of life and death and immortality, a bird flew in through an unglazed window, circled the hall in its flight, and flew out once more into the darkness of the night.

The Christian priest bade the king see in the flight of the bird within the hall the transitory life of man, and claimed for his faith that it showed the soul, in passing from the hall of life, winging its way not into the darkness of night, but into the sunlit radiance of a more glorious world.

Annie Besant (1847-1933)

Chartless

I never saw a moor,
I never saw the sea;
Yet know I how the heather looks,
And what a wave must be.

I never spoke with God,
Nor visited in heaven;
Yet certain am I of the spot
As if the chart were given.

Emily Dickinson (1830-1886)

Here is a greater miracle

Tell me this instinct for immortality is a nightmare, an excrescence bred of ignorance. I reply that here is a greater miracle than the one you displace. The law of correspondence is broken.

No; when I find a fossil, and on it I find fossil fins, I rightly infer that the fossil was once a fish, and there must have been water to match it, correspond with it. The eye, with its coats, humours, lens, and retina, is impossible without light to match it; the bird, with its wings beautifully formed, must have air with buoyancy to match it.

So when I find this instinct for immortality as universal as language, as old as human thought, as real as consciousness, as deep as human needs, and as high as human aspiration, I reply it seems to me it must have life beyond to match it, to equalise it, to make the music plain, and fill the earth with law, and the universe with justice.

We believe in justice; we believe in hope; but if there is no future life, there can be no justice in the universe. The girl dies outraged in the gutter, the betrayer goes free, the scales are never adjusted.
I believe in God, because I believe in justice, in love, and in hope.

A J Waldron

Belief

The pain we have to suffer seems so broad,
Set side-by-side with this life's narrow span,
We need no greater evidence that God
Has some diviner destiny for man.

He would not deem it worth His while to send
Such crushing sorrows as pursue us here,
Unless beyond this fleeting journey's end
Our chastened spirits found another sphere

So small this world! So vast its agonies!
A future life is needed to adjust
These ill-proportioned, wide discrepancies
Between the spirit and its frame of dust.

So when my soul writhes with some aching grief,
And all my heart-strings tremble at the strain,
My Reason lends new courage to Belief,
And all God's hidden purposes seem plain.

Ella Wheeler Wilcox (1850-1919)

Love will not cease

The nature of love suggests a future life. Love though undefinable is none the less a mighty power.

Love will not cease from following after the loved one; death is no barrier to it. The mother sees the body of her darling child laid in the grave, but the tender mother love will cross the chasm and dwell with her child on the other side.

Love is as reliable as any other faculty of the soul. What the reason is to the intellect, love is to the heart; one is as reliable as the other.

True love cannot believe that death ends all.

T. Ewing Duffield

The beauty of death

Let me sleep, for my soul is intoxicated with love, and
Let me rest, for my spirit has had its bounty of days and nights...
...Place me upon clusters of leaves and
Carry me upon your friendly shoulders and walk slowly to the
deserted forest...
Take from me all earthly raiment and place me deep in my
Mother Earth; and place me with care upon my mother's breast.
Cover me with soft earth, and let each handful be mixed
With seeds of jasmine, lilies, and myrtle; and when they
Grow above me and thrive on my body's element, they will
Breathe the fragrance of my heart into space;
And reveal even to the Sun the secret of my Peace;
And sail with the breeze and comfort the wayfarer...

I have passed a mountain peak and my soul is soaring in the
Firmament of complete and unbound freedom;
I am far, far away my companions, and the clouds are
Hiding the hills from my eyes...
The songs of the waves and the hymns of the streams are scattered.
And the voices of the throngs reduced to silence;
And I can hear naught but the music of Eternity
In exact harmony with the Spirit's desires.
I am cloaked in full whiteness;
I am in comfort; I am in Peace.

Kahlil Gibran (1883-1931)

Nature proclaims a resurrection

In nature there are many things which seem to die but have continued life. Nature proclaims a resurrection.

What is night but the death of the day? And morning but the day's resurrection? What is winter but the year putting on her shroud and remaining under the embrace of death until spring, with her dewy fingers and warm zephyrs, returns to resurrect her?

The changes which take place all around us are very suggestive of a resurrection of the dead. The leafless tree of winter will be clothed anew with leaves, flowers, and fruit when spring returns; the unsightly apparently lifeless worm in its cell will soon change into a beautiful butterfly brilliant with colours.

The power of the resurrection is exemplified in a worm. Shall man, so fearfully and wonderfully made, have the spirit cast out forever?

T. Ewing Duffield

End and beginning are dreams

Never the spirit was born; the spirit shall cease to be never;
Never was time it was not;
End and Beginning are dreams!
Birthless and deathless and changeless remaineth the spirit for
ever;
Death hath not touched it at all, dead though the house of it seems!
Who knoweth it exhaustless, self-sustained,
Immortal, indestructible, shall such say, I have killed a man, or
caused to kill?
Nay, but as when one layeth his worn-out robes away,
And, taking new ones, sayeth, these will I wear to-day!
So putteth by the spirit lightly its garb of flesh,
And passeth to inherit a residence afresh.

The Bhagavad Gita

Meditation XVII

All mankind is of one author, and is one volume; when one man dies, one chapter is not torn out of the book, but translated into a better language; and every chapter must be so translated; God employs several translators; some pieces are translated by age, some by sickness, some by war, some by justice; but God's hand is in every translation, and his hand shall bind up all our scattered leaves again, for that library where every book shall lie open to one another; as therefore the bell that rings to a sermon, calls not upon the preacher only, but upon the congregation to come; so this bell calls us all: but how much more me, who am brought so near the door by this sickness.

No man is an island, entire of itself; every man is a piece of the continent, a part of the main; if a clod be washed away by the sea, Europe is the less, as well as if a promontory were, as well as if a manor of thy friend's or of thine own were; any man's death diminishes me, because I am involved in mankind, and therefore never send to know for whom the bell tolls; it tolls for thee.

John Donne (1572-1631)

Kontakion

Give rest, O Christ, to Thy servant with Thy saints:
Where sorrow and pain are no more;
Neither sighing but life everlasting.
Thou only art immortal, the creator and maker of man:
And we are mortal formed from the dust of the earth,
And unto earth shall we return:
For so Thou didst ordain,
When Thou created me saying:
'Dust thou art and unto dust shalt thou return.'
All we go down to the dust;
And weeping o'er the grave we make our song:
Alleluia, alleluia, alleluia.

Traditional Byzantine hymn

Peace is here now

You are wrong in thinking of peace as something which is to come only in a future life. There is no reason for expecting it hereafter but its having begun now. Every true surrender of selfish principles to God and the inward monitor is the beginning of heaven and heaven's peace.

The best proof of a heaven to come is its dawning in us now. We are blinded by common errors to the degree of celestial good which is to be found on earth. I do not tell you to labour for it; for a selfish impatience may remove it from us. I would say, accept your inward and outward trials as appointed by the Friend of your soul for its progress and perfection, and use them for this end, not doubtingly or impetuously, but confidingly; and just as fast as the power of Christian virtue grows within you, peace and heaven will come, unless, for some greater good, present happiness be obstructed by physical causes.

Be of good cheer. Be not weary in well doing. Be not anxious.

William Ellery Channing (1780-1842)

All is well

Death is nothing at all,
I have only slipped into the next room
I am I and you are you
Whatever we were to each other, that we are still.
Call me by my old familiar name,
Speak to me in the easy way which you always used
Put no difference in your tone,
Wear no forced air of solemnity or sorrow
Laugh as we always laughed at the little jokes we enjoyed together.
Play, smile, think of me, pray for me.
Let my name be ever the household world that it always was,
Let it be spoken without effect, without the trace of shadow on it.
Life means all that it ever meant.
It it the same as it ever was, there is unbroken continuity.
Why should I be out of mind because I am out of sight?
I am waiting for you, for an interval, somewhere very near,
Just around the corner.
All is well.

Canon Henry Scott Holland (1847-1918)

Immortality in miniature

The consciousness of existence is the only conceivable idea we have of another life, and the continuance of that consciousness is immortality. The consciousness of existence, of the knowing that we exist, is not necessarily confined to the same form, nor to the same matter, even in this life. We have not in all cases the same form, nor in any case the same matter that composed our bodies twenty or thirty years ago; and yet we are conscious of being the same persons.

That the consciousness of existence is not dependent on the same form or the same matter is demonstrated to our senses in the works of the creation, as far as our senses are capable of receiving that demonstration. A very numerous part of the animal creation preaches to us, far better than Paul, the belief of a life hereafter. Their little life resembles an Earth and a heaven—a present and a future state, and comprises, if it may be so expressed, immortality in miniature.

The most beautiful parts of the creation to our eye are the winged insects, and they are not so originally. They acquire that form and that inimitable brilliancy by progressive changes. The slow and creeping caterpillar-worm of today passes in a few days to a torpid figure and a state resembling death; and in the next change comes forth in all the miniature magnificence of life, a splendid butterfly. No resemblance of the former creature remains; everything is changed; all his powers are new, and life is to him another thing.

Thomas Paine (1737-1809)

It is not death to die

It is not death to die,
To leave this weary road,
And, midst the brotherhood on high,
To be at home with God.

It is not death to close
The eye long dimmed by tears,
And wake in glorious repose,
To spend eternal years.

It is not death to bear
The wrench that sets us free
From dungeon-chain, to breathe the air
Of boundless liberty.

It is not death to fling
Aside this sinful dust,
And rise on strong, exulting wing,
To live among the just.

Jesus, thou Prince of Life,
Thy chosen cannot die!
Like Thee, they conquer in the strife,
To reign with Thee on high.

George Washington Bethune (1805-1862)

The fear of death can never enter your heart

So live your life that the fear of death can never enter your heart. Trouble no one about their religion; respect others in their view, and demand that they respect yours.

Love your life, perfect your life, beautify all things in your life. Seek to make your life long and its purpose in the service of your people. Prepare a noble death song for the day when you go over the great divide.

Always give a word or a sign of salute when meeting or passing a friend, even a stranger, when in a lonely place. Show respect to all people and grovel to none. When you arise in the morning give thanks for the food and for the joy of living. If you see no reason for giving thanks, the fault lies only in yourself.

Abuse no one and no thing, for abuse turns the wise ones to fools and robs the spirit of its vision. When it comes your time to die, be not like those whose hearts are filled with the fear of death, so that when their time comes they weep and pray for a little more time to live their lives over again in a different way.

Sing your death song and die like a hero going home.

Chief Tecumseh (1768-1813)

A happy man

When these graven lines you see,
Traveller, do not pity me;
Though I be among the dead,
Let no mournful word be said.

Children that I leave behind,
And their children, all were kind;
Near to them and to my wife,
I was happy all my life.

My three sons I married right,
And their sons I rocked at night;
Death nor sorrow never brought
Cause for one unhappy thought.

Now, and with no need of tears,
Here they leave me, full of years,—
Leave me to my quiet rest
In the region of the blest.

Edward Arlington Robinson (1869-1935)

From **Meditation XVIII**

His soul is gone, whither? Who saw it come in, or who saw it go out? Nobody; yet everybody is sure he had one, and hath none.

If I will ask mere philosophers what the soul is, I shall find amongst them that will tell me, it is nothing but the temperament and harmony, and just and equal composition of the elements in the body, which produces all those faculties which we ascribe to the soul; and so in itself is nothing, no separable substance that overlives the body.

They see the soul is nothing else in other creatures, and they affect an impious humility to think as low of man. But if my soul were no more than the soul of a beast, I could not think so; that soul that can reflect upon itself, consider itself, is more than so.

This soul this bell tells me is gone out, whither? Who shall tell me that? I know not who it is, much less what he was, the condition of the man, and the course of his life, which should tell me whither he is gone, I know not. I was not there in his sickness, nor at his death; I saw not his way nor his end, nor can ask them who did, thereby to conclude or argue whither he is gone.

But yet I have one nearer me than all these, mine own charity; I ask that, and that tells me he is gone to everlasting rest, and joy, and glory.

John Donne (1572-1631)

Prospice

Fear death?—to feel the fog in my throat,
The mist in my face,
When the snows begin, and the blasts denote
I am nearing the place,
The power of the night, the press of the storm,
The post of the foe;
Where he stands, the Arch Fear in a visible form,
Yet the strong man must go:
For the journey is done and the summit attained,
And the barriers fall,
Though a battle's to fight ere the guerdon be gained,
The reward of it all.
I was ever a fighter, so—one fight more,
The best and the last!
I would hate that death bandaged my eyes and forbore,
And bade me creep past.
No! let me taste the whole of it, fare like my peers
The heroes of old,
Bear the brunt, in a minute pay glad life's arrears
Of pain, darkness and cold.
For sudden the worst turns the best to the brave,
The black minute's at end,
And the elements' rage, the fiend-voices that rave,
Shall dwindle, shall blend,
Shall change, shall become first a peace out of pain,
Then a light, then thy breast,
O thou soul of my soul! I shall clasp thee again,
And with God be the rest!

Robert Browning (1812–1889)

Griefs are our glory

The human soul is purified and exalted by a trial and grief. Life itself has a new charm for him who has trodden its depths as well as its heights.

The keenness of our suffering increases the intensity of our joy. Yes, there is a meaning in tears, a discipline in darkness, and our griefs are our glory.

Therefore, when your dearest hopes are disappointed, when your faith in man is tried by bitterest ingratitude, or you are cast upon the bed of sickness, oh, do not despair!

For these are the divine processes by which your nobler self is developed, by which the crude bullion of your nature, purified in the flames of tribulation, is freshly minted with the image and superscription of a perfect manhood.

Charles W Wendte (1844-1931)

Lux est umbra Dei

Nay, Death, thou art a shadow! Even as light
Is but the shadow of invisible God,
And of that shade the shadow is thin Night,
Veiling the earth whereon our feet have trod;
So art Thou but the shadow of this life,
Itself the pale and unsubstantial shade
Of living God, fulfill'd by love and strife
Throughout the universe Himself hath made:
And as frail Night, following the flight of earth,
Obscures the world we breathe in, for a while,
So Thou, the reflex of our mortal birth,
Veilest the life wherein we weep and smile:
But when both earth and life are whirl'd away,
What shade can shroud us from God's deathless day?

John Addington Symonds (1840–93)

Today we live, tomorrow we die

Very soon your life here will end; consider, then, what may be in store for you elsewhere. Today we live; tomorrow we die and are quickly forgotten. Oh, the dullness and hardness of a heart which looks only to the present instead of preparing for that which is to come!

Therefore, in every deed and every thought, act as though you were to die this very day. If you had a good conscience you would not fear death very much. It is better to avoid sin than to fear death. If you are not prepared today, how will you be prepared tomorrow? Tomorrow is an uncertain day; how do you know you will have a tomorrow?

What good is it to live a long life when we amend that life so little? Indeed, a long life does not always benefit us, but on the contrary, frequently adds to our guilt. Would that in this world we had lived well throughout one single day. Many count up the years they have spent in religion but find their lives made little holier. If it is so terrifying to die, it is nevertheless possible that to live longer is more dangerous. Blessed is he who keeps the moment of death ever before his eyes and prepares for it every day.

How happy and prudent is he who tries now in life to be what he wants to be found in death. Perfect contempt of the world, a lively desire to advance in virtue, a love for discipline, the works of penance, readiness to obey, self-denial, and the endurance of every hardship for the love of Christ, these will give a man great expectations of a happy death.

Thomas a Kempis (c.1380-1471)

To death

Come not in terrors clad, to claim
An unresisting prey:
Come like an evening shadow, Death!
So stealthily, so silently!
And shut mine eyes, and steal my breath;
Then willingly, O willingly,
With thee I'll go away!

What need to clutch with iron grasp
What gentlest touch may take?
What need with aspect dark to scare,
So awfully, so terribly,
The weary soul would hardly care,
Call'd quietly, call'd tenderly,
From thy dread power to break?

'Tis not as when thou markest out
The young, the blest, the gay,
The loved, the loving—they who dream
So happily, so hopefully;
Then harsh thy kindest call may seem,
And shrinkingly, reluctantly,
The summon'd may obey.

But I have drunk enough of life—
The cup assign'd to me
Dash'd with a little sweet at best,
So scantily, so scantily —
To know full well that all the rest
More bitterly, more bitterly,
Drugg'd to the last will be.

And I may live to pain some heart
That kindly cares for me:
To pain, but not to bless. O Death!
Come quietly—come lovingly —
And shut mine eyes, and steal my breath;
Then willingly, O willingly,
I'll go away with thee!

Caroline Southey (1787–1854)

The wealth of love

From the background of pain and sorrow often break out the noblest and most winning manifestations of humanity. The depth of human sympathy, the wealth of its love, is displayed in scenes of tribulation and need.

The robes of charity show their whiteness amid the gloom of poverty and distress. Christlike patience is born of suffering, the soul shines out in its essential splendour through the medium of bodily anguish, and faith trims her lamp in the shadow of the grave.

Shall we call this existence a trivial thing, whose very miseries are the occasions of the noblest triumphs, whose trials may be converted into divine strength, whose tears may change into celestial dew, and nourish flowers of immortal hope?

Edwin H Chapin (1814-1880)

Dominus illuminatio mea

In the hour of death, after this life's whim,
When the heart beats low, and the eyes grow dim,
And pain has exhausted every limb —
The lover of the Lord shall trust in Him.

When the will has forgotten the lifelong aim,
And the mind can only disgrace its fame,
And a man is uncertain of his own name—
The power of the Lord shall fill this frame.

When the last sigh is heaved, and the last tear shed,
And the coffin is waiting beside the bed,
And the widow and child forsake the dead—
The angel of the Lord shall lift this head.

For even the purest delight may pall,
And power must fail, and the pride must fall,
And the love of the dearest friends grow small —
But the glory of the Lord is all in all.

Anonymous, 18th cent.

The last and crowning joy

What then is our help? How then shall we reconcile ourselves to life? Only by throwing ourselves, as Christ did, when sorrows of this kind came upon him, out of ourselves into love of God, and into love of man. This is one secret of victory over suffering, loss of self in love of God.

But that alone would not have been enough for Jesus. For such solitary communion tends to isolate us with ourselves. Jesus, and we with him, must lose himself in communion with God through work of love done to mankind.

He passed from his own trouble into active help, and forgot all pain in the larger thoughts of what he might do to heal and succour pain.

I think some of us might try that way.

Trouble, anxiety, discontent, double themselves by brooding on them; they lessen to a shred when we seek the anxious, the troubled and the discontented, and lift them up, using our pain to help their pain. It is by work of this kind that the vast conception of mankind growing through sorrow and sacrifice into union with God slowly arises in us, and dwarfs in the end all our personal distress.

We may, with Him, feel the very worst agony of life, and know we can live no more. But if, in the midst of it, we live in love, if still, for all the pain, we lose ourselves, we shall win the last and crowning joy of death for love.

Stopford A Brooke (1832-1916)

After death

When I forth fare beyond this narrow earth,
With all its metes and bounds of now and here,
And brooding clouds of ignorance and fear
That overhung me on my day of birth,
Where through the jocund sun's perennial mirth
Has shone more inly bright each coming year
With some new glory of that outer sphere
Where length and breadth and height are little worth,
Then shall I find that even here below
We guessed the secret of eternity,
And learned in years the yearless mystery;
For in our earliest world we came to know
The master-lesson and the riddle's key:
Unending love unending growth shall be.

Charles Francis Richardson

This tranquil mystery

Through all the mysteries of our earthly lot, we would feel ourselves embosomed in the Infinite Strength and Peace. Whether we walk in the morning light, or in the night shadows, over, around, and beneath us are spread the Everlasting Arms.

How strong is the assurance that what is bound up with our life, and makes a dear part of our being, cannot be wholly lost; that it must answer to the love in which it is more deeply than ever enshrined! How real becomes the unseen world, no longer unfamiliar, but warm with the treasures and light of home!

How we look through its half-opened gates, into its glory and its peace, where the innocence and beauty of childhood must dwell in the life of which they are the image; and the ties that here seem broken must be preserved in the love that made them ours; and the powers we would have trained here, must be unfolded in the same care that inspired our striving, and will not let it be in vain.

Nor would we forget that by this tranquil mystery which we call death, we are brought the closer to a sense of an infinite calm of unchangeable good in which we must confide; on whose bosom, with our beloved that have fallen asleep therein, we can rest, sure of compensations flowing from the Life that can comprehend the depth of these affections it has implanted, and the bitterness of earthly loss.

Samuel Johnson (1709-1784)

Absence

What shall I do with all the days and hours
That must be counted ere I see thy face?
How shall I charm the interval that lo'wers
Between this time and that sweet time of grace?

I'll tell thee: for thy sake, I will lay hold
Of all good aims, and consecrate to thee,
In worthy deeds, each moment that is told
While thou, beloved one, art far from me.

For thee, I will arouse my thoughts to try
All heavenward flights, all high and holy strains;
For thy dear sake, I will walk patiently
Through these long hours, nor call their minutes pains.

I will this weary blank of absence make
A noble task-time, and will therein strive
To follow excellence, and to o'ertake
More good than I have won since yet I live.

So may this darksome time build up in me
A thousand graces which shall thus be thine;
So may my love and longing hallowed be,
And thy dear thought an influence divine.

Frances Anne Kemble (1809-1893)

There is no death

There is an 'unseen universe' lying over against and within that which is visible and apparent to the senses. The outer, the visible, is in a state of constant whirl and change; it may be resolved back into its original elements, or dissipated in impalpable gases; but the universe of life and principles in which man finds his consciousness, his freedom, his real self- hood, is not and cannot be affected by any of these outer changes.

Man may sum up in himself all there is of nature below him; but this is not his full measure; he is more; he is a spirit; he has a moral nature; he has free-will. And thus man, though a part of nature, and with a body conditioned in natural laws, has a something beyond this, and hence he may give back his body to the earth, and yet himself live on in his finer, his real world of spirit...

Life is a fact, a persistent energy, making possible and holding all there is in thought, in beauty, in love, in joy. Death is a nonentity, a nothing; or only a passing phase, or an appearance. 'God is not the God of the dead but of the living', of life; and hence, in the world of the real there is no death.

H W Thomas (1832-1909)

On the death of my son Charles

My son, thou wast my heart's delight,
Thy morn of life was gay and cheery;
That morn has rushed to sudden night,
Thy father's house is sad and dreary.

I held thee on my knee, my son!
And kissed thee laughing, kissed thee weeping;
But ah! thy little day is done,
Thou 'rt with thy angel sister sleeping.

The staff, on which my years should lean,
Is broken, ere those years come o'er me;
My funeral rites thou shouldst have seen,
But thou art in the tomb before me.

Thou rear'st to me no filial stone,
No parent's grave with tears beholdest;
Thou art my ancestor, my son!
And stand'st in Heaven's account the oldest.

On earth my lot was soonest cast,
Thy generation after mine,
Thou hast thy predecessor past;
Earlier eternity is thine.

I should have set before thine eyes
The road to Heaven, and showed it clear;
But thou untaught spring'st to the skies,
And leav'st thy teacher lingering here.

Sweet Seraph, I would learn of thee,
And hasten to partake thy bliss!
And oh! to thy world welcome me,
As first I welcomed thee to this.

Dear Angel, thou art safe in heaven;
No prayers for thee need more be made;
Oh! let thy prayers for those be given
Who oft have blessed thy infant head.

My father! I beheld thee born,
And led thy tottering steps with care;
Before me risen to Heaven's bright morn,
My son! My father! Guide me there.

Daniel Webster (1782-1852)

Is our lost friend still mysteriously here?

The curtains of yesterday drop down, the curtains of to-morrow roll up; but yesterday and to-morrow both are. Pierce through the Time-Element, glance into the Eternal. And seest thou therein any glimpse of Immortality?

Is the white tomb of our loved one, who died from our arms, and must be left behind us there, which rises in the distance, like a pale, mournfully receding milestone, to tell how many toilsome, uncheered miles we have journeyed on alone, but a pale spectral illusion?

Is our lost friend still mysteriously here, even as we are here mysteriously, with God? Know of a truth that only the Time-shadows have perished, or are perishable; that the real being of whatever was, and whatever is, and whatever will be, is even now and forever.

Thomas Carlyle (1795-1881)

Death

Death, thou wast once an uncouth hideous thing,
Nothing but bones,
The sad effect of sadder groans:
Thy mouth was open, but thou couldst not sing.

For we considered thee as at some six
Or ten years hence,
After the loss of life and sense,
Flesh being turned to dust, and bones to sticks.

We looked on this side of thee, shooting short;
Where we did find
The shells of fledge souls left behind,
Dry dust, which sheds no tears, but may extort.

But since our Saviour's death did put some blood
Into thy face,
Thou art grown fair and full of grace,
Much in request, much sought for as a good.

For we do now behold thee gay and glad,
As at Doomsday;
When souls shall wear their new array,
And all thy bones with beauty shall be clad.

Therefore we can go die as sleep, and trust
Half that we have
Unto an honest faithful grave;
Making our pillows either down, or dust.

George Herbert (1593-1633)

Immortal hope

No one can be reasoned or persuaded into any living faith in God or immortality, any more than reason and persuasion can draw from the cold April furrow the field of waving wheat. The faith *grows* in the individual and in the race, under that culture to which the higher powers subject us, — a culture in which the elements are experience and fidelity, thought and action, love and loss, aspiration and achievement. Love and Loss, the sweetest angel and the sternest one, join their hands to give us that gift of the immortal hope.

If one asks, 'how shall I gain faith in God and hope of immortality?' What better answer can we give him than this: Be faithful, live, and love! Work and love press their treasures on you with full hands. Open your eyes to the glory of the universe. Watch the world's new life quickening in bud and bird-song. Get into sympathetic current with the hearts around you. Be sincere; be a man. Keep open-minded to all knowledge, and keep humble in the sense of your ignorance.

In your darkest hour, set yourself to brighten another's life. Be patient. If an oak-tree takes a century to get its growth, shall a man expect to win his crown in a day? Find what word of prayer you can sincerely say, and say it with your heart. Look at the moral meanings of things. Learn to feel through your own littleness that higher power out of which comes all the good in you. Join yourself to men wherever you can find them in that noblest attitude, true worship of a living God. Know that to mankind are set two teachers of immortality, and see to it that you so faithfully learn of Love that Sorrow when she comes shall perfect the lesson.

George S Merriam (1803-1880)

There shall be more joy

The little angels of Heaven
Each wear a long white dress,
And in the tall arcadings
Play ball and play at chess;

With never a soil on their garments,
Not a sigh the whole day long,
Not a bitter note in their pleasure,
Not a bitter note in their song.

But they shall know keener pleasure,
And they shall know joy more rare—
Keener, keener pleasure
When you, my dear, come there.

The little angels of Heaven
Each wear a long white gown,
And they lean over the ramparts
Waiting and looking down.

Ford Madox Ford (1873-1939)

A noble soul goes home

Love in its simplest and most common forms is often strangely wise. Many a mother learns from the light of her baby's eyes more than all wisdom of books can teach. When the little, unconscious thing is taken from her arms, there is given to her sometimes a feeling, 'My baby is *mine* forever;' a feeling in whose presence we stand in reverent, tender awe.

It is not every experience of bereavement which brings with it this uplift of comfort. But to the noble love of a noble object there comes the sense of something in the beloved that outlasts death.

To the *noble* love, for most of our affection has a selfish strain in it; the clinging to another for what of present enjoyment he yields to us brings small illumination or assurance. But as self loses itself in another's life, there comes to us the deep instinct of something over which death has no power.

Above all, when we unselfishly love one in whom dwells moral nobility, —when it is a great and vital and holy nature to which we join ourselves, —there comes to us a profound and pregnant sense of its immortality. It is when death's stroke has fallen that that sense rises into full, triumphant bloom.

No wonder the disciples felt that their Master lived! Theirs was the experience that in substance repeats itself whenever from among those who love it a noble soul goes home.

George S Merriam (1803-1880)

A prospect of heaven makes death easy

There is a land of pure delight
Where saints immortal reign;
Infinite day excludes the night,
And pleasures banish pain.

There everlasting spring abides,
And never-withering flowers;
Death like a narrow sea divides
This heavenly land from ours.

Sweet fields beyond the swelling flood
Stand dressed in living green:
So to the Jews old Canaan stood,
While Jordan rolled between.

But timorous mortals start and shrink
To cross this narrow sea,
And linger shivering on the brink,
And fear to launch away.

Oh could we make our doubts remove,
These gloomy doubts that rise,
And see the Canaan that we love,
With unbeclouded eyes;

Could we but climb where Moses stood
And view the landscape o'er,
Not Jordan's stream, nor death's cold flood,
Should fright us from the shore.

Isaac Watts (1674-1748)

Nothing ever falls away

We think about the things in this world that we have never seen much as we believe in the things of the other world.

… I shall know, I think, better than I have ever known, how real the things may be that lie upon that other side, to which men cross but once, and come not back, nor send to us with stories of their travel. I shall be able to think that life and love, like the planet, are round; and that though we lose them out of our little horizon, nothing that holds to them by the eternal gravitation ever falls away.

…I shall feel, too, how certain it must be, after all, that from out that heavenly morning, sweet words and breaths are sent back into our waiting twilights, writings are made in our hearts of the blessed things that they walk in the midst of, in that near, fair Other Side.

Adeline Dutton Train Whitney (1824-1906)

Peace! What do tears avail?

Peace! what do tears avail?
She lies all dumb and pale,
And from her eye
The spirit of lovely life is fading,
And she must die!
Why looks the lover wroth? The friend upbraiding?
Reply, reply!

Hath she not dwelt too long
'Midst pain, and grief, and wrong?
Then, why not die?
Why suffer again her doom of sorrow,
And hopeless lie?
Why nurse the trembling dream until to-morrow?
Reply, reply!

Death! Take her to thine arms,
In all her stainless charms,
And with her fly
To heavenly haunts, where, clad in brightness,
The Angels lie.
Wilt bear her there, O Death! In all her whiteness?
Reply, reply!

Barry Cornwall (1787–1874)

The heart of man

Look, then, at the heart of man, see how vast a thing is human love. Conceive of it in any form you please, the love of family, the love of father, child, wife, friends; or the love of art, or glory, or country, or mankind. Whence comes that marvellous force of love? It is not the object which creates the love, for the heart may set itself upon an unworthy object, and the object which to one seems loveliest may possess no attractions for others.

It is the love which clothes the object with ideal loveliness. Nothing shows more strikingly than this fact that we are something in ourselves that we do not depend entirely upon our senses, and upon the outer world. Look above at that soul which lavishes itself without one thought of self, which only lives and breathes for the happiness of another, which thinks no sacrifice too great, which cannot be disenchanted, which death cannot rob altogether, which even treachery and contempt cannot alienate, which sheds all its treasures of affection on a deformed body, a sickly spirit, an ungrateful heart.

Is that mighty force of love no more than the flame of a candle which at last goes out in the socket? Nay more, when rising above the works of God to God Himself, love fastens itself immediately on the supreme object of love, shall it be frustrated in its hopes? Shall that love, at once so holy and so strong, be for ever shattered by death? Shall God never show himself? Shall God never give Himself? Shall that which seemed the most real thing in life, prove only to be a deception and a torture?

No, the heart of man prophesies his immortality.

J J Stewart Perowne (1823-1904)

Resignation

There is no flock, however watched and tended,
But one dead lamb is there!
There is no fireside, howsoe'er defended,
But has one vacant chair!

The air is full of farewells to the dying,
And mournings for the dead;
The heart of Rachel, for her children crying,
Will not be comforted!

Let us be patient! These severe afflictions
Not from the ground arise,
But oftentimes celestial benedictions
Assume this dark disguise.

We see but dimly through the mists and vapours;
Amid these earthly damps
What seem to us but sad, funereal tapers
May be heaven's distant lamps.

There is no Death! What seems so is transition;
This life of mortal breath
Is but a suburb of the life elysian,
Whose portal we call Death.

She is not dead,—the child of our affection,—
But gone unto that school
Where she no longer needs our poor protection,
And Christ himself doth rule.

In that great cloister's stillness and seclusion,
By guardian angels led,
Safe from temptation, safe from sin's pollution,
She lives, whom we call dead,

Day after day we think what she is doing
In those bright realms of air;
Year after year, her tender steps pursuing,
Behold her grown more fair.

Thus do we walk with her, and keep unbroken
The bond which nature gives,
Thinking that our remembrance, though unspoken,
May reach her where she lives.

Not as a child shall we again behold her;
For when with raptures wild
In our embraces we again enfold her,
She will not be a child;

But a fair maiden, in her Father's mansion,
Clothed with celestial grace;
And beautiful with all the soul's expansion
Shall we behold her face.

And though at times impetuous with emotion
And anguish long suppressed,
The swelling heart heaves moaning like the ocean,
That cannot be at rest,—

We will be patient, and assuage the feeling
We may not wholly stay;
By silence sanctifying, not concealing,
The grief that must have way.

Henry Wadsworth Longfellow (1807–1882)

Death never touches love

Eternal life is in us *now*, in proportion as we are unselfish, as we believe in invisible things, as we love what is outside of self, as we care for things which are spiritual. We are all two-sided, double-natured. By one nature we are allied to the visible world and love material things. That is well, if it does not go too far.

But by the other nature we are akin to the Infinite Soul that lives in the world, the Invisible Spirit that dwells in the visible universe, immortal, eternal. In proportion as we feel that life in us we are immortal and can believe in immortality.

Death never touches love, integrity, faith. We all feel this, and we show that we feel it when we find comfort in whatever of goodness we can find in the lives that have gone from us.

No money, no worldly success, no personal beauty, will so comfort those we shall leave behind us as the good we have done, the respect we have earned, the sweetness and nobleness that were in our souls. The reason is that while the life to come is too vague a thing to be imagined in detail, men feel sure that immortal qualities on earth are the pledge of immortal life in heaven.

These are the treasures laid up in heaven which neither moth nor rust, neither death nor the ruin of the universe, can corrupt or take away.

Rev William H Lyon

Beyond the veil

They are all gone into the world of light!
And I alone sit lingering here;
Their very memory is fair and bright,
And my sad thoughts doth clear.

It glows and glitters in my cloudy breast,
Like stars upon some gloomy grove,
Or those faint beams in which this hill is drest,
After the sun's remove.

I see them walking in an air of glory,
Whose light doth trample on my days;
My days, which are at best but dull and hoary,
Mere glimmerings and decays.

O holy Hope, and high Humility,
High as the heavens above!
These are your walks, and you have showed them me,
To kindle my cold love.

Dear, beauteous Death! the jewel of the just,
Shining nowhere but in the dark,
What mysteries do lie beyond thy dust,
Could Man outlook that mark!

He that hath found some fledged bird's nest, may know
At first sight, if the bird be flown;
But what fair well or grove he sings in now,
That is to him unknown.

And yet, as Angels in some brighter dreams
Call to the soul when man doth sleep,
So some strange thoughts transcend our wonted themes,
And into glory peep.

If a star were confined into a tomb,
Her captive flames must needs burn there;
But when the hand that locked her up, gives room,
She'll shine through all the sphere.

O Father of eternal life, and all
Created glories under Thee!
Resume Thy spirit from this world of thrall
Into true liberty.

Either disperse these mists, which blot and fill
My perspective still, as they pass;
Or else remove me hence unto that hill
Where I shall need no glass.

Henry Vaughan (1622–1695)

All is divine harmony

On no subject are our ideas more warped and pitiable than on death. Instead of the sympathy, the friendly union, of life and death so apparent in Nature, we are taught that death is an accident, a deplorable punishment for the oldest sin, the arch-enemy of life, etc...

But let children walk with Nature, let them see the beautiful blendings and communions of death and life, their joyous inseparable unity, as taught in woods and meadows, plains and mountains and streams of our blessed star, and they will learn that death is stingless indeed, and as beautiful as life, and that the grave has no victory, for it never fights.

All is divine harmony.

John Muir (1838–1914)

For us

If we have not learned that God's in man,
And man in God again,
That to love thy God is to love thy brother,
And to serve thy God is to serve each other—
Then Christ was born in vain!

If we have not learned that one man's life
In all men lives again;
That each man's battle, fought alone,
Is won or lost for everyone
Then Christ hath lived in vain!

If we have not learned that death's no break
In life's unceasing chain,
That the work in one life well begun
In others is finished, by others is done—
Then Christ hath died in vain!

If we have not learned of immortal life,
And a future free from pain,
The Kingdom of God in the heart of man,
And the living world on heaven's plan—
Then Christ arose in vain!

Charlotte Perkins Gilman (1860-1935)

The universal consciousness

A man may set himself against all such beliefs in the 'Hereafter.' He may make believe not to believe, but he does not thereby rid himself of this universal consciousness. His rational self wars against his unbelief. His attitude of unbelief is not only un-Biblical, but wholly unphilosophical as well.

Socrates, when asked where he would choose to be buried, made reply: 'Bury me where you will, if you can catch me.' There you have the wisdom of the wisest of ancient philosophers.

Like Job of old, he declined to entertain the conception that Death was the extinction of consciousness. 'Though after the flesh worms destroy the body' was a fact present to the mind of Socrates as well as to that of Job. But he did not infer from it that there was 'Nothingness after Death.'

Monsignor Robert Hugh Benson (1871-1914)

Eternity

On this wondrous sea,
Sailing silently,
Ho! Pilot, ho!
Knowest thou the shore
Where no breakers roar,
Where the storm is o'er?

In the silent west
Many sails at rest,
Their anchors fast;
Thither I pilot thee,—
Land, ho! Eternity!
Ashore at last!

Emily Dickinson (1830-1886)

Fear nothing

There is no exemption to be won from suffering, none from fear. Pain, weakness, bereavement, death, — these things must come, and we must sometimes tremble before them, — no divine hand will pluck them away.

But in our fear we learn a deeper strength. These are the gifts with which Life answers our faithful service. The brave, the gentle, the peace-makers, the pure in heart, the forgiving, the patient, the heroic, are blessed, — incomparably enriched. This is what we know of the relation of the One Power to ourselves, — that it asks the very highest and best we can give, and returns our service with the best and highest we can receive. This is what that power we name God is to us.

So of the mystery of death. The veil is not lifted, but it stirs before the breath of our prayers and hopes. The deepest fear in man is the fear of death, and that fear is conquered in him by something greater than itself. Even on the natural plane man is seldom afraid of death when it comes; it is rather the distant image that appals him. Before the reality some instinct seems to bid him not to fear. Every noble sentiment lifts men above the dread of death. For their country on the battlefield, for other men in sudden accidents and perils, men give their lives instinctively or deliberately.

It is personal love to which death seems to menace irretrievable and final disaster. But it is personal love to which comes the divinest presage. Some voice says to our yearning heart, 'Fear nothing, doubt nothing, only *live!*' From our birth to our death we are encompassed by mystery, but it is a mystery which may, if we will have it so, grow warm, luminous, divine.

George S Merriam (1803-1880)

I long for household voices gone

I long for household voices gone,
For vanished smiles I long,
But God hath led my dear ones on,
And he can do no wrong.

I know not what the future hath
Of marvel or surprise,
Assured alone that life and death
His mercy underlies.

And if my heart and flesh are weak
To bear an untried pain,
The bruised reed He will not break,
But strengthen and sustain.

And so beside the Silent Sea
I wait the muffled oar;
No harm from Him can come to me
On ocean or on shore.

I know not where His islands lift
Their fronded palms in air;
I only know I cannot drift
Beyond His love and care.

John Greenleaf Whittier (1807-1892)

The essence of what we loved

We talk of immortality; but there is a better phrase than that, the word of Jesus, 'Eternal Life.' That implies not mere duration, but quality. It blends the present and the future in one. It sets before us a state into which we are called to enter now, and into which as we enter we find ourselves at home in our Father's house, beyond the power of doubt and fear.

The hope of immortality — the assurance of some good beyond, — is born from a sense of the value of life. Life is felt to be precious as it is consecrated by the moral struggle in ourselves, and as it is viewed in others with sympathy. We give our moral effort and our sympathy, and these are encountered by the tremendous play of human joys and sorrows, and the result is a sense of life as intensely significant.

The feeling of communion with Christ, with angels and saints, — its natural basis is the reverence and love for great souls. As such reverence and love is deep, and as death removes the objects, the sense of a continued communion arises spontaneously. No form of our consciousness is more vivid and profound than this. It has a background of mystery, — mystery scarcely deeper or other than that which envelops the earthly love. *What* do I love in the friend whom here I see? Is it the individuality, or that higher power of which it transmits a ray?

The sense of this blending of the human and divine does not weaken or perplex our affection for the friend we see; it intensifies and sublimates it. So, in the sense of communion with the unseen friend, it disturbs us not that we cannot say how much is there of the remembered personality, how much of the one eternal deity. The essence of what we loved and love is sure and undying.

George S Merriam (1803-1880)

The sleep

Of all the thoughts of God that are
Borne inward into souls afar,
Along the Psalmist's music deep,
Now tell me if that any is
For gift or grace surpassing this —
'He giveth His beloved, sleep'?

What would we give to our beloved?
The hero's heart to be unmoved,
The poet's star-tun'd harp to sweep,
The patriot's voice to teach and rouse,
The monarch's crown to light the brows?—
He giveth His beloved, sleep.

What do we give to our beloved?
A little faith all undisproved,
A little dust to overweep,
And bitter memories to make
The whole earth blasted for our sake:
He giveth His beloved, sleep.

'Sleep soft, beloved!' we sometimes say
Who have no tune to charm away
Sad dreams that through the eyelids creep:
But never doleful dream again
Shall break the happy slumber when
He giveth His beloved, sleep.

O earth, so full of dreary noises!
O men, with wailing in your voices!
O delved gold, the wailers heap!
O strife, O curse, that o'er it fall!
God strikes a silence through you all,
And giveth His beloved, sleep.

His dews drop mutely on the hill,
His cloud above it saileth still,
Though on its slope men sow and reap:
More softly than the dew is shed,
Or cloud is floated overhead,
He giveth His beloved, sleep.

Ay, men may wonder while they scan
A living, thinking, feeling man
Confirm'd in such a rest to keep;
But angels say, and through the word
I think their happy smile is heard—
'He giveth His beloved, sleep.'

For me, my heart that erst did go
Most like a tired child at a show,
That sees through tears the mummers leap,
Would now its wearied vision close,
Would childlike on His love repose
Who giveth His beloved, sleep.

And friends, dear friends, when it shall be
That this low breath is gone from me,
And round my bier ye come to weep,
Let One, most loving of you all,
Say, 'Not a tear must o'er her fall!
He giveth His beloved, sleep.'

Elizabeth Barrett Browning (1806–61)

A Unitarian prayer

Grant unto us, Almighty God, that we, feeling toward Thee as children, may trust where we cannot see, and hope where all seems doubtful, ever looking unto Thee as our Father that doeth all things well, our Father that ordereth all.

Thus, knowing that all things are in Thy hands, may we abide Thy time, patiently doing the work thou hast given us to do.

Mercifully give us peace in the hour of death, and afterward an abundant entrance into the life eternal. Amen.

Unitarian Service Book (1903)

I would not live alway

I would not live alway — live alway below!
Oh no, I'll not linger when bidden to go:
The days of our pilgrimage granted us here
Are enough for life's woes, full enough for its cheer:
Would I shrink from the path which the prophets of God,
Apostles, and martyrs, so joyfully trod?
Like a spirit unblest, o'er the earth would I roam,
While brethren and friends are all hastening home?

I would not live alway: I ask not to stay
Where storm after storm rises dark o'er the way;
Where seeking for rest we but hover around,
Like the patriarch's bird, and no resting is found;
Where Hope, when she paints her gay bow in the air,
Leaves its brilliance to fade in the night of despair,
And joy's fleeting angel ne'er sheds a glad ray,
Save the gleam of the plumage that bears him away.

I would not live alway—thus fettered by sin,
Temptation without and corruption within;
In a moment of strength if I sever the chain,
Scarce the victory's mine, ere I 'm captive again;
E'en the rapture of pardon is mingled with fears,
And the cup of thanksgiving with penitent tears:
The festival trump calls for jubilant songs,
But my spirit her own *miserere* prolongs.

I would not live alway — no, welcome the tomb,
Since Jesus hath lain there I dread not its gloom;
Where He deigned to sleep, I'll too bow my head,
All peaceful to slumber on that hallowed bed.
Then the glorious daybreak, to follow that night,
The orient gleam of the angels of light,
With their clarion call for the sleepers to rise
And chant forth their matins, away to the skies.

Who, who would live alway? Away from his God,
Away from yon heaven, that blissful abode,
Where the rivers of pleasure flow o'er the bright plains,
And the noontide of glory eternally reigns;
Where the saints of all ages in harmony meet,
Their Saviour and brethren transported to greet,
While the songs of salvation exultingly roll
And the smile of the Lord is the feast of the soul.

That heavenly music! What is it I hear?
The notes of the harpers ring sweet in mine ear!
And see, soft unfolding those portals of gold,
The King all arrayed in His beauty behold!
Oh give me, oh give me, the wings of a dove,
To adore him—be near him—enwrapt with His love;
I but wait for the summons, I list for the word—
Alleluia—Amen—evermore with the Lord!

William Augustus Muhlenberg (1796-1877)

Trained as God's children

Death? This is only one stage of our career. We are here at school; we learn our lessons or we do not; we attain the ends we seek after or we only partly attain them or do not attain them at all; and then we go on.

Does that mean that it ends there? I do not believe it. I believe that it simply means that we go out into a larger opportunity, from the planet to the system, to the galaxy, to the universe, wider knowledge answering to more magnificent resources in the infinite universe.

We, with undeveloped powers that may increase and advance forever, and a universe so complete, so exhaustless, that it may match and lure and lead and rejoice us forever; we being trained as God's children in God's likeness and helping others to attain the same magnificent ends, this I believe to be the significance, the meaning, the purpose, of life.

Ephraim Emerton (1851-1935)

Vital spark of heav'nly flame

Vital spark of heav'nly flame!
Quit, O quit this mortal frame:
Trembling, hoping, ling'ring, flying,
O the pain, the bliss of dying!
Cease, fond Nature, cease thy strife,
And let me languish into life.

Hark! they whisper; angels say,
Sister Spirit, come away!
What is this absorbs me quite?
Steals my senses, shuts my sight,
Drowns my spirits, draws my breath?
Tell me, my soul, can this be death?

The world recedes; it disappears!
Heav'n opens on my eyes! My ears
With sounds seraphic ring!
Lend, lend your wings! I mount! I fly!
O Grave! where is thy victory?
O Death! where is thy sting?

Alexander Pope (1688-1744)

The eternal cycle

We have heard much in these days of a kind of universal immortality. We are reminded of the analogies of all organic life. The tree does not die. It passes into other forms of life, which in their turn give place to new and ever new combinations of elements.

We are shown the eternal cycle of the sea, the cloud, the fertilizing rain, the earth, and again the sea, and we are told: Thus it is with the life of man. It, too, can never die, but is taken up into the universal life. Its material parts go back into the eternal round of Nature, from which they sprang.

But what of its spiritual part, the only part that here really interests us? This, too, we are told lives on forever. Every human thought or word or action has its permanent effect upon the aggregate of human experience. No particle of this spiritual activity of man is wasted, any more than is any particle of the activity of Nature.

Character, — the accumulation of spiritual qualities that constitutes the real man, — this never dies, but goes on influencing the world of human being and through this affecting even the world of matter to the remotest verge of time. And this is immortality. The individual soul lives in the truest sense in its unending influence upon the universal life.

Ephraim Emerton (1851-1935)

Death

Calm Death, God of crossed hands and passionless eyes,
Thou God that never heedest gift nor prayer,
Men blindly call thee cruel, unaware
That everything is dearer since it dies.
Worn by the chain of years, without surprise,
The wise man welcomes thee, and leaves the glare
Of noisy sunshine gladly, and his share
He chose not in mad life and windy skies.
Passions and dreams of love, the fever and fret
Of toil, seem vain and petty when we gaze
On the imperious Lords who have no breath:
Atoms or worlds,—we call them lifeless, yet
In thy unending peaceful day of days
They are divine, all-comprehending Death.

George Pellew (1793-1866)

The exaltation of life

Wherefore should man doubt of life and immortality? Are they not clearly revealed to the soul that loves the true life? Being passes through its phases, but it does not cease to be.

A dark soul not recognizing its root in the Godhead may be troubled at the changes in nature, and made sad by the passing away of that which to it alone seems real.

But is not all death in nature birth? In death itself visibly appears the exaltation of life. There is no destructive principle in nature, for nature throughout is free and unclouded life.

It is not death which kills, but the new life concealed behind death begins to develop itself. Death and birth are but the struggle of life with itself to assume a more glorious and congenial form.

John Hunt (1827-1907)

Sonnet 55

Not marble, nor the gilded monuments
Of princes, shall outlive this powerful rhyme;
But you shall shine more bright in these contènts
Than unswept stone, besmeared with sluttish time.

When wasteful war shall statues overturn,
And broils root out the work of masonry,
Nor Mars his sword nor war's quick fire shall burn
The living record of your memory.

'Gainst death and all-oblivious enmity
Shall you pace forth; your praise shall still find room
Even in the eyes of all posterity
That wear this world out to the ending doom.

So, till the judgment that yourself arise,
You live in this, and dwell in lovers' eyes.

William Shakespeare (1564-1616)

Their righteousness has not been forgotten

There be some who have left a name behind them, whose remembrance is sweet as honey in all mouths.

And there be some who have no memorial, who are perished as though they had never been.

But their righteousness has not been forgotten, and the glory of their work cannot be blotted out.

Their bodies are buried in peace, but their name liveth for evermore.

The people will tell of their wisdom, and the congregation will show forth their praise.

For the memorial of virtue is immortal, because it is known with God and with men.

When it is present men take example of it, and when it is gone they earnestly desire it.

It weareth a crown, and triumpheth for ever; having gotten the victory striving for undefiled rewards.

The righteous shall be in everlasting remembrance, and the memory of the just shall be blessed.

Though a good life hath but few days, yet a good name endureth for ever.

Though the righteous be overtaken by death, they shall be at rest; their souls are in the hand of God.

Unitarian Service Book (1903)

The secret of the world

It is the secret of the world that all things subsist and do not die, but only retire a little from sight and afterwards return again.

Nothing is dead; men feign themselves dead, and endure mock funerals and mournful obituaries, and there they stand looking out of the window, sound and well, in some new strange disguise.

Jesus is not dead; he is very well alive; nor John, nor Paul, nor Mahomet, nor Aristotle; at times we believe we have seen them all, and could easily tell the names under which they go.

Ralph Waldo Emerson (1803-1882)

He sendeth sun, he sendeth shower

He sendeth sun, he sendeth shower,
Alike they're needful for the flower:
And joys and tears alike are sent
To give the soul fit nourishment.
As comes to me or cloud or sun,
Father! Thy will, not mine, be done!
Can loving children e'er reprove
With murmurs whom they trust and love?
Creator! I would ever be
A trusting, loving child to Thee:
As comes to me or cloud or sun,
Father! Thy will, not mine, be done!
Oh, ne'er will I at life repine:
Enough that thou hast made it mine.
When falls the shadow cold of death
I yet will sing, with parting breath,
As comes to me or shade or sun,
Father! Thy will, not mine, be done!

Sarah Fuller Flower Adams (1805-1848)

To know the eternal

To know the eternal is the immortality we enjoy. But to know the eternal we must forget about ourselves. We must cease to be consumed by a cancerous anxiety to endure in time and be permanent in space. In the order of Nature our own particular lives are of no especial importance. And unless we recognize this, we are necessarily doomed to a miserable fate.

We must recognize that our mere selves can never give us ultimate fulfilment or blessedness of soul. Only by losing ourselves in Nature or God can we escape the wretchedness of finitude and find the final completion and salvation of our lives.

This, the free man understands. He knows how insignificant he is in the order of Nature. But he also knows that if only he can lose himself in Nature or God then, in his own insignificant particularity, the eternal and infinite order of Nature can be displayed. For in the finite is the infinite expressed, and in the temporal, the eternal.

It is this knowledge that makes man free, that breaks the finite fetters from his soul enabling him to embrace the infinite and to possess eternity.

Joseph Ratner (1927)

On the death of a young lady of five years of age

From dark abodes to fair etherial light
Th' enraptur'd innocent has wing'd her flight;
On the kind bosom of eternal love
She finds unknown beatitude above.

This known, ye parents, nor her loss deplore,
She feels the iron hand of pain no more;
The dispensations of unerring grace,
Should turn your sorrows into grateful praise;

Let then no tears for her henceforward flow,
No more distress'd in our dark vale below,
Her morning sun, which rose divinely bright,
Was quickly mantled with the gloom of night;

But hear in heav'n's blest bow'rs your Nancy fair,
And learn to imitate her language there.
'Thou, Lord, whom I behold with glory crown'd,
By what sweet name, and in what tuneful sound

Wilt thou be prais'd? Seraphic pow'rs are faint
Infinite love and majesty to paint.
To thee let all their graceful voices raise,
And saints and angels join their songs of praise.'

Perfect in bliss she from her heav'nly home
Looks down, and smiling beckons you to come;
Why then, fond parents, why these fruitless groans?
Restrain your tears, and cease your plaintive moans.

Freed from a world of sin, and snares, and pain,
Why would you wish your daughter back again?
No—bow resign'd. Let hope your grief control,
And check the rising tumult of the soul.

Calm in the prosperous, and adverse day,
Adore the God who gives and takes away;
Eye him in all, his holy name revere,
Upright your actions, and your hearts sincere,

Till having sail'd through life's tempestuous sea,
And from its rocks, and boist'rous billows free,
Yourselves, safe landed on the blissful shore,
Shall join your happy babe to part no more.

Phillis Wheatley (1753-1784)

A Unitarian prayer

Lord of our life and Disposer of our lot! Inspire us, we pray Thee, with a divine faith in the loftiness and eternity of our lives; subdue us to the waiting trust and lowly patience of those who have lived as fellow-workers with thee; and most of all of Him whose victory over death is the prophecy of our triumph, if only like Him we lay hold of eternal life.

Day by day, remembering that our time is short, may we grow in faith, in self-denial, in charity, in heavenly-mindedness; in the purity by which we may see Thee; and the surrender which makes us one with Thee.

And then, mingle us at last with our loved ones, and with the mighty host of Thy redeemed for evermore. Amen.

Unitarian Service Book (1903)

Spirits of the dead

Thy soul shall find itself alone
'Mid dark thoughts of the grey tomb-stone;
Not one, of all the crowd, to pry
Into thine hour of secrecy.

Be silent in that solitude,
Which is not loneliness- for then
The spirits of the dead, who stood
In life before thee, are again
In death around thee, and their will
Shall overshadow thee; be still.

The night, though clear, shall frown,
And the stars shall not look down
From their high thrones in the Heaven
With light like hope to mortals given,
But their red orbs, without beam,
To thy weariness shall seem
As a burning and a fever
Which would cling to thee for ever.

Now are thoughts thou shalt not banish,
Now are visions ne'er to vanish;
From thy spirit shall they pass
No more, like dew-drop from the grass.

The breeze, the breath of God, is still,
And the mist upon the hill
Shadowy, shadowy, yet unbroken,
Is a symbol and a token.
How it hangs upon the trees,
A mystery of mysteries!

Edgar Allan Poe (1809-1849)

Nothing is lost

Whence is this universe — this existence — which is the cause of all sorrow? We do not know...We only know the round of existence — the circle of phenomena. We plant a seed, from it springs a tree; the tree bears fruit, the fruit bears a seed; from the seed springs again a tree; or a bird lays an egg, from it arises another bird, this bird lays another egg, from it arises again a bird: and so it is with the world, and with all worlds. They have come from earlier worlds, and these from others that were earlier still.

Existence unfolds itself, forms appear and disappear, but being remains unchanged. Life succeeds life, but nothing is lost and nothing is gained. Being is a circle that has neither beginning nor end. As the moisture is drawn up into the clouds, and poured down upon the earth, to be drawn up again by the sun's rays; so being undergoes its perpetual and manifold evolutions in the midst of which it remains unchanged.

One individual falls here, and one there; but others rise to replace these, and thus the procession advances in a circle which never ends.

John Hunt (1827-1907)

At that hour

At that hour when all things have repose,
O lonely watcher of the skies,
Do you hear the night wind and the sighs
Of harps playing unto Love to unclose
The pale gates of sunrise?

When all things repose, do you alone
Awake to hear the sweet harps play
To Love before him on his way,
And the night wind answering in antiphon
Till night is overgone?

Play on, invisible harps, unto Love,
Whose way in heaven is aglow
At that hour when soft lights come and go,
Soft sweet music in the air above
And in the earth below.

James Joyce (1882 - 1941)

The inevitable order

The spiritual life Jesus taught was not a thing of another world. It was the life of the spirit shared by every man that cometh into the world — not every man that goes out of the world.

The Kingdom of God He sought to establish was the reign of righteousness in the lives of men here and now. The resurrection He cared about was the deliverance of the soul of man from the slavery of sin into the freedom of the law of righteousness.

The ascension that He promised was no stage-exit into an impossible heaven, but the rising of the individual soul into harmony with the inevitable order that is the soul of the universe of God.

Ephraim Emerton (1851-1935)

Early death

She passed away like morning dew
Before the sun was high;
So brief her time, she scarcely knew
The meaning of a sigh.

As round the rose its soft perfume,
Sweet love around her floated;
Admired she grew-while mortal doom
Crept on, unfeared, unnoted.

Love was her guardian Angel here,
But Love to Death resigned her;
Though Love was kind, why should we fear
But holy Death is kinder?

Hartley Coleridge (1796-1849)

Peculiar glory

To the sensible appearances of death, so sad and appalling, we should do well to oppose the energy of soul with which it is often encountered. Then death itself will furnish us with a proof of immortality.

Sometimes the hour of death is an hour of peculiar glory for human nature. Instead of being conquered, man is seen to conquer the last foe; and he seems to suffer only that the greatness of humanity may be developed. In instances like these, the last act of the soul is an assertion of its immortality.

Can we believe that this moment of sublime virtue is the moment of annihilation, — that the soul is extinguished when its beauty is most resplendent? If God intended that death should be an eternal extinction, would it be adorned, as it often is, with a radiance of the noblest, loveliest sentiments and affections of our nature? Would the greatest triumph of man be the harbinger of his ruin?

William Ellery Channing (1780-1842)

Even such is time

Even such is Time, that takes in trust
Our youth, our joys, our all we have,
And pays us but with earth and dust;
Who in the dark and silent grave
When we have wandered all our ways,
Shuts up the story of our days;
But from this earth, this grave, this dust,
My God shall raise me up, I trust.

Sir Walter Raleigh (1554-1618)

Wherever they may be

Let us not, then, imagine that the usefulness of the good is finished at death. Then rather does it begin. Let us not judge of their state by associations drawn from the chillness and silence of the grave.

They have gone to abodes of life, of warmth, of action. They have gone to fill a larger place in the system of God. Death has expanded their powers. The clogs and fetters of the perishable body have fallen off, that they may act more freely and with more delight in the grand system of creation.

We should represent them to our minds as ascended to a higher rank of existence, and admitted to cooperate with far higher communities. This earth was only their school, their place of education, where we saw their powers comparatively in an infant state. They have now reached a maturer age, and are gone to sustain more important relations. They have been called because their agency was needed in higher services than those of this world.

Where they are now acting, it is not given to us to know...But wherever they may be, they are more useful, more honourably occupied, than when on earth; and by following their steps, we may, however separated from them during life, hope to obtain admission into the same bright regions where they are pressing onward to perfection.

William Ellery Channing (1780-1842)

Farewell

Farewell to thee! But not farewell
To all my fondest thoughts of thee;
Within my heart they still shall dwell
And they shall cheer and comfort me.

Life seems more sweet that thou didst live
And men more true that thou wert one;
Nothing is lost that thou didst give,
Nothing destroyed that thou hast done.

Anne Bronte (1820-1849)

High flight

Oh! I have slipped the surly bonds of earth
And danced the skies on laughter-silvered wings;
Sunward I've climbed, and joined the tumbling mirth
Of sun-split clouds — and done a hundred things
You have not dreamed of — wheeled and soared and swung
High in the sunlit silence. Hov'ring there,
I've chased the shouting wind along, and flung
My eager craft through the footless halls of air.
Up, up the long, delirious burning blue
I've topped the windswept heights with easy grace
Where never lark, or even eagle flew.
And, while with silent, lifting mind I've trod
The high untrespassed sanctity of space,
Put out my hand, and touched the face of God.

Pilot Officer John Gillespie Magee RCAF (1922-1941)

The surest pledge

Nothing is so completely beyond the power of death as a noble love. Parting can shatter only its outward shell. Under that strange touch, love in its inmost recesses kindles and glows with a diviner life.

Whom of the living do we love as we love our dead? Whom else do we hold so sacredly and so surely? Not as a memory of a lost past, — nothing in our present is so real as they, and toward our unknown future we go with a great and solemn gladness, beckoned by their presence. Through them duty is most sacred to us, in them we are strong to labour and endure, and for their sake we learn to love all others.

It is the sense of them mingling with a beauty that makes the earth glow to our eyes with the light that never was on sea or land It is their love that becomes to us the surest pledge and deepest experience of the goodness of God.

Love slain by death? It does not come to its full stature till death's hand is laid upon it. Its bond is but half-tested till it spans the gulf between the seen and unseen worlds. Its service is incomplete till it has vanquished in our hearts the fear of the grave, and taught us how death is swallowed up in victory.

George S Merriam (1803-1880)

He that is down needs fear no fall

He that is down needs fear no fall,
He that is low, no pride;
He that is humble ever shall
Have God to be his guide.

I am content with what I have,
Little be it or much;
And, Lord, contentment will I crave,
Because Thou savest such.

Fullness to such a burden is
That go on pilgrimage:
Here little, and hereafter bliss,
Is best from age to age.

John Bunyan (1628-1688)

If I should never see the moon again

If I should never see the moon again
Rising red gold across the harvest field
Or feel the stinging soft rain
As the brown earth her treasures yield.

If I should never taste the salt sea spray
As the ship beats her course across the breeze.
Or smell the dog-rose and new-mown hay,
Or moss or primroses beneath the tree.

If I should never hear the thrushes wake
Long before the sunrise in the glimmering dawn.
Or watch the huge Atlantic rollers break
Against the rugged cliffs in baffling scorn.

If I have to say goodbye to stream and wood,
To wide ocean and the green clad hill,
I know that He, who made this world so good
Has somewhere made a heaven better still.

This bears witness with my latest breath
Knowing the love of God,
I fear no death.

Major Malcolm Boyd (died 1944)

I thank Thee God, that I have lived

I thank Thee God, that I have lived
In this great world and known its many joys:
The songs of birds, the strongest sweet scent of hay,
And cooling breezes in the secret dusk;
The flaming sunsets at the close of day,
Hills and the lovely, heather-covered moors;
Music at night, and the moonlight on the sea,
The beat of waves upon the rocky shore
And wild white spray, flung high in ecstasy;
The faithful eyes of dogs, and treasured books,
The love of Kin and fellowship of friends
And all that makes life dear and beautiful.

I thank Thee too, that there has come to me
A little sorrow and sometimes defeat,
A little heartache and the loneliness
That comes with parting and the words 'Good-bye';
Dawn breaking after weary hours of pain,
When I discovered that night's gloom must yield
And morning light break through to me again.
Because of these and other blessings poured
Unasked upon my wondering head,
Because I know that there is yet to come
An even richer and more glorious life,
And most of all, because Thine only Son
Once sacrificed life's loveliness for me,
I thank Thee, God, that I have lived.

Elizabeth Craven (1750-1828)

In memoriam **(Part XXVII)**

I envy not in any moods,
The captive void of noble rage,
The linnet born within the cage,
That never knew the summer woods:

I envy not the beast that takes
His license in the field of time,
Unfetter'd by the sense of crime,
To whom a conscience never wakes;

Nor, what may count itself as blest,
The heart that never plighted troth
But stagnates in the weed of sloth;
Nor any want-begotten rest.

I hold it true, whate'er befall;
I feel it, when I sorrow most;
'Tis better to have loved and lost
Than never to have loved at all.

Alfred, Lord Tennyson, Poet Laureate (1809-1892)

Life

Life, believe, is not a dream
So dark as sages say;
Oft a little morning rain
Foretells a pleasant day.
Sometimes there are clouds of gloom,
But these are transient all;
If the shower will make the roses bloom,
O why lament its fall?

Rapidly, merrily
Life's sunny hours flit by,
Gratefully, cheerily,
Enjoy them as they fly!

What though Death at times steps in
And calls our best away?
What though sorrow seems to win,
O'er hope, a heavy sway?
Yet hope again elastic springs,
Unconquered, though she fell;
Still buoyant are her golden wings,
Still strong to bear us well.
Manfully, fearlessly,
The day of trial bear,
For gloriously, victoriously,
Can courage quell fear!

Charlotte Bronte (1816-1855)

Peace, my heart

Peace, my heart, let the time for the parting be sweet.
Let it not be a death but completeness.
Let love melt into memory and pain into songs.
Let the flight through the sky end in the folding of the wings over the nest.
Let the last touch of your hands be gentle like the flower of the night.
Stand still, O Beautiful End, for a moment, and say your last words in silence.
I bow to you and hold up my lamp to light your way.

Rabindranath Tagore (1861-1941)

The soldier

If I should die, think only this of me:
That there's some corner of a foreign field
That is for ever England. There shall be
In that rich earth a richer dust concealed;
A dust whom England bore, shaped, made aware,
Gave, once, her flowers to love, her ways to roam,
A body of England's, breathing English air,
Washed by the rivers, blest by suns of home.

And think, this heart, all evil shed away,
A pulse in the eternal mind, no less
Gives somewhere back the thoughts by England given;
Her sights and sounds; dreams happy as her day;
And laughter, learnt of friends; and gentleness,
In hearts at peace, under an English heaven.

Rupert Brooke (1887-1915)

Songs of the death of children

You must not shut the night inside you,
But endlessly in light the dark immerse.
A tiny lamp has gone out in my tent –
I bless the flame that warms the universe.

Friedrich Ruckert (1788-1866)

They that love beyond the world

They that love beyond the world cannot be separated by it,
Death cannot kill what never dies.
Nor can spirits ever be divided that love
And live in the same divine principle,
The root and record of their friendship.
If absence be not death, neither is theirs.
Death is but crossing the world, as friends do the seas;
They live in one another still.
For they must needs be present,
That love and live in that which is omnipresent.
In this divine glass, they see face to face;
And their converse is free as well as pure.
This is the comfort of friends,
That though they may be said to die,
Yet their friendship and society are,
In the best sense, ever present, because immortal.

William Penn (1644-1718)

The new life's salutation

Life, we've been long together
Through pleasant and through cloudy weather;
'Tis hard to part when friends are dear,
Perhaps 'twill cost a sigh, a tear;
Then steal away, give little warning,
Choose thine own time:
Say not 'Good night,' but in some brighter clime
Bid me 'Good morning.'

Anna Barbauld (1743-1825)

When at heart you should be sad

When at heart you should be sad,
Pondering the joys we had,
Listen and keep very still.
If the lowing from the hill
Or the toiling of a bell
Do not serve to break the spell,
Listen: you may be allowed
To hear my laughter from a cloud.

Sir Walter Raleigh (1554-1618)

To a desolate friend

O friend, like some cold wind to-day
Your message came, and chilled the light;
Your house so dark, and mine so bright,—
I could not weep, I could not pray!

My wife and I had kissed at morn,
My children's lips were full of song;
O friend, it seemed such cruel wrong,
My life so full, and yours forlorn!

We slept last night clasped hand in hand,
Secure and calm—and never knew
How fared the lonely hours with you,
What time those dying lips you fanned.

We dreamed of love, and did not see
The shadow pass across our dream;
We heard the murmur of a stream,
Not death's for it ran bright and free.

And in the dark her gentle soul
Passed out, but oh! we knew it not!
My babe slept fast within her cot,
While yours woke to the slow bell's toll.

She paused a moment,—who can tell?—
Before our windows, but we lay
So deep in sleep she went away,
And only smiled a sad farewell!

It would be like her; well we know
How oft she waked while others slept—
She never woke us when she wept,
It would be like her thus to go!

Ah, friend! you let her stray too far
Within the shadow-haunted wood,
Where deep thoughts never understood
Breathe on us and like anguish are.

One day within that gloom there shone
A heavenly dawn, and with wide eyes
She saw God's city crown the skies,
Since when she hasted to be gone.

Too much you yielded to her grace;
Renouncing self, she thus became
An angel with a human name,
And angels coveted her face.

Earth's door you set so wide, alack
She saw God's gardens, and she went
A moment forth to look; she meant
No wrong, but oh! she came not back!

Dear friend, what can I say or sing,
But this, that she is happy there?
We will not grudge those gardens fair
Where her light feet are wandering.

The child at play is ignorant
Of tedious hours; the years for you
To her are moments: and you too
Will join her ere she feels your want.

The path she wends we cannot track:
And yet some instinct makes us know
Hers is the joy, and ours the woe,—
We dare not wish her to come back!

William James Dawson (b. 1854)

On death

Then Almitra spoke, saying, We would ask now of death.

And he said: You would know the secret of death. But how shall you find it unless you seek it in the heath of life? The owl whose night-bound eyes are blind unto the day cannot unveil the mystery of light. If you would indeed behold the spirit of death, open your heart wide unto the body of life. For life and death are one, even as the river and sea are one.

In the depth of your hopes and desires lies your silent knowledge of the beyond; and like seeds dreaming beneath the snow your heart dreams of spring. Trust the dreams, for in them is hidden the gate to eternity.

Your fear of death is but the trembling of the shepherd when he stands before the king whose hand is to be laid upon him in honour. Is the shepherd not joyful beneath his trembling, that he shall wear the mark of the king? Yet is he not more mindful of his trembling?

For what is it to die but to stand naked in the wind and to melt into the sun? And what is it to cease breathing, but to free the breath from its restless tides, that it may rise and expand and seek God unencumbered?

Only when you drink from the river of silence shall you indeed sing. And when you have reached the mountain top, then you shall begin to climb. And when the earth shall claim your limbs, then shall you truly dance.

Kahlil Gibran (1883-1931)

If death is kind

Perhaps if death is kind, and there can be returning,
We will come back to earth some fragrant night,
And take these lanes to find the sea, and bending
Breathe the same honeysuckle, low and white.

We will come down at night to these resounding beaches
And the long gentle thunder of the sea,
Here for a single hour in the wide starlight
We shall be happy, for the dead are free.

Sara Teasdale (1884-1933)

The dying Christian to his soul

Vital spark of heav'nly flame!
Quit, O quit this mortal frame:
Trembling, hoping, ling'ring, flying,
O the pain, the bliss of dying!
Cease, fond Nature, cease thy strife,
And let me languish into life.

Hark! they whisper; angels say,
Sister Spirit, come away!
What is this absorbs me quite?
Steals my senses, shuts my sight,
Drowns my spirits, draws my breath?
Tell me, my soul, can this be death?

The world recedes; it disappears!
Heav'n opens on my eyes! my ears
With sounds seraphic ring!
Lend, lend your wings! I mount! I fly!
O Grave! where is thy victory?
O Death! where is thy sting?

Alexander Pope (1688–1744)

The undiscovered country

Could we but know
The land that ends our dark, uncertain travel,
Where lie those happier hills and meadows low,—
Ah, if beyond the spirit's inmost cavil,
Aught of that country could we surely know,
Who would not go?

Might we but hear
The hovering angels' high imagined chorus,
Or catch, betimes, with wakeful eyes and clear,
One radiant vista of the realm before us,—
With one rapt moment given to see and hear,
Ah, who would fear?

Were we quite sure
To find the peerless friend who left us lonely,
Or there, by some celestial stream as pure,
To gaze in eyes that here were lovelit only,—
This weary mortal coil, were we quite sure,
Who would endure?

Edmund Clarence Stedman (1833–1906)

The secret place

There is a safe and secret place
Beneath the wings divine,
Reserv'd for all the heirs of grace:
Oh, be that refuge mine!

The least and feeblest there may bide
Uninjur'd and unaw'd;
While thousands fall on every side,
He rests secure in God.

The angels watch him on his way,
And aid with friendly arm;
And Satan, roaring for his prey,
May hate, but cannot harm.

He feeds in pastures large and fair
Of love and truth divine;
O child of God, O glory's heir,
How rich a lot is thine!

A hand almighty to defend,
An ear for every call,
An honour'd life, a peaceful end,
And heaven to crown it all!

Henry Francis Lyte (1793–1847)

The way to heaven

Heaven is open every day;
In night also
He that would wend his upward way
May surely go.
There is no wall to that demesne
Where God resides; nor any screen
To hide the glories of that scene,—
If man will know.

The ladder which the Hebrew saw
Whenas he slept,
From earth God never doth updraw,
But still hath kept;
And angels ever to and fro
On errands swiftly glide and glow,—
For love above, for love below,
Its rounds have stept.

Thereon the saint doth daily mount
Above the stars,
Caring nowhit to take account
Of earthly bars;
Since well 'tis known to such as he
There are no guards but pass him free;
He hath the watchword and the key,
In peace, or wars.

Charles Goodrich Whiting (1842-1922)

Bereavement

Nay, weep not, dearest, though the child be dead;
He lives again in Heaven's unclouded life,
With other angels that have early fled
From these dark scenes of sorrow, sin, and strife.
Nay, weep not, dearest, though thy yearning love
Would fondly keep for earth its fairest flowers,
And e'en deny to brighter realms above
The few that deck this dreary world of ours:
Though much it seems a wonder and a woe
That one so loved should be so early lost,
And hallowed tears may unforbidden flow
To mourn the blossom that we cherished most,
Yet all is well; God's good design I see,
That where our treasure is, our hearts may be!

John Godfrey Saxe (1816–1887)

Life and death

O ye who see with other eyes than ours,
And speak with tongues we are too deaf to hear,
Whose touch we cannot feel yet know ye near,
When, with a sense of yet undreamed-of powers,
We sudden pierce the cloud of sense that lowers,
Enwrapping us as 't were our spirit's tomb,
And catch some sudden glory through the gloom,
As Arctic sufferers dream of sun and flowers!
Do ye not sometimes long for power to speak
To our dull ears, and pierce their should of clay
With a loud cry, 'Why, then, this grief at "death"?
We are the living, you the dead to-day!
This truth you soon shall see, dear hearts, yet weak,
In God's bright mirror cleared from mortal breath!'

Lilla Cabot Perry (1848-1933)

The sunset is nearing

Seek to make life henceforth a consecrated thing; that so, when the sunset is nearing, with its murky vapours and lowering skies, the very clouds of sorrow may be fringed with golden light.

Thus will the song in the house of your pilgrimage be always the truest harmony. It will be composed of no jarring, discordant notes; but with all its varied tones will form one sustained, life-long melody; dropped for a moment in death, only to be resumed with the angels, and blended with the everlasting cadences of your Father's house.

John Ross MacDuff (1818-1895)

Immortal

How living are the dead!
Enshrined, but not apart,
How safe within the heart
We hold them still our dead,
Whatever else be fled!
Our constancy is deep
Toward those who lie asleep
Forgetful of the strain and mortal strife
That are so large a part of this, our earthly life.
They are our very own
From them from them alone
Nothing can us estrange,
Nor blight autumnal, no, nor wintry change.
The midnight moments keep a place for them
And though we wake to weep
They are beside us still in joy, in pain
In every crucial hour, they come again
Angelic from above
Bearing the gifts of blessing and of love
Until the shadowy path, they lonely trod
Becomes for us a bridge,
That upwards leads to God.

Florence Earle Coates (1850-1927)

Canticle of the sun

O most high, almighty, good Lord God, to Thee belong praise, glory, honour, and all blessing!

Praised be my Lord God with all His creatures; and specially our brother the sun, who brings us the day, and who brings us the light; fair is he, and shining with a very great splendour: O Lord, to us he signifies Thee!

Praised be my Lord for our sister the moon, and for the stars, the which He has set clear and lovely in heaven.

Praised be my Lord for our brother the wind, and for air and cloud, calms and all weather, by the which Thou upholdest in life all creatures.

Praised be my Lord for our sister water, who is very serviceable unto us, and humble, and precious, and clean.

Praised be my Lord for our brother fire, through whom Thou givest us light in the darkness; and he is bright, and pleasant, and very mighty, and strong.

Praised be my Lord for our mother the earth, the which doth sustain us and keep us, and bringeth forth divers fruits, and flowers of many colours, and grass.

Praised be my Lord for all those who pardon one another for His love's sake, and who endure weakness and tribulation; blessed are they who peaceably shall endure, for Thou, O most Highest, shalt give them a crown!

Praised be my Lord for our sister, the death of the body, from whom no man escapeth. Woe to him who dieth in mortal sin!

Blessed are they who are found walking by Thy most holy will, for the second death shall have no power to do them harm.

Praise ye, and bless ye the Lord, and give thanks unto Him, and serve Him with great humility.

St Francis of Assisi (1182-1226) Tr. by Matthew Arnold (1822-1888)

Thank God

Thank God for life!
E'en though it bring much bitterness and strife,
And all our fairest hopes be wrecked and lost,
E'en though there be more ill than good in life,
We cling to life and reckon not the cost.
Thank God for life!

Thank God for love!
For though sometimes grief follows in its wake,
Still we forget love's sorrow in love's joy,
And cherish tears with smiles for love's dear sake;
Only in heaven is bliss without alloy.
Thank God for love!

Thank God for pain!
No tear hath ever yet been shed in vain,
And in the end each sorrowing heart shall find
No curse, but blessings in the hand of pain;
Even when he smiteth, then is God most kind.
Thank God for pain!

Thank God for death!
Who touches anguished lips and stills their breath
And giveth peace unto each troubled breast;
Grief flies before thy touch, O blessed death;
God's sweetest gift; thy name in heaven is Rest.
Thank God for death!

Unknown

The eternal arms

What a power has death to awe and hush the voices of this earth! How mute we stand when that presence confronts us, and we look upon the silence he has wrought in a human life!

We can only gaze, and bow our heads, and creep with our broken, stammering utterances under the shelter of some great word which God has spoken, and in which we see through the history of human sorrow the outstretching and overshadowing of the eternal arms.

W W Battershall

Resurrection

If it be all for naught, for nothingness
At last, why does God make the world so fair?
Why spill this golden splendour out across
The western hills, and light the silver lamp
Of eve? Why give me eyes to see, and soul
To love so strong and deep? Then, with a pang
This brightness stabs me through, and wakes within
Rebellious voice to cry against all death?
Why set this hunger for eternity
To gnaw my heartstrings through, if death ends all?
If death ends all, then evil must be good,
Wrong must be right, and beauty ugliness.
God is a Judas who betrays His son,
And with a kiss, damns all the world to hell,
If Christ rose not again.

Unknown

This is heaven

O, to have the soul bathed all day long in this thought, 'as the pebble in the willow brook' until the words come like the tears, because the heart is full, and we cannot help it; to feel, in the darkest hour, that there is an unseen spectator whose eyes rest on us like morning on the flowers; and that in the severest sorrow, we can sink into a presence full of love and sympathy, deeper than ever breathed from earth or sky or loving hearts—a presence in which all fears and anxieties melt away as ice-crystals in the warm ocean.

This is heaven.

Edward Thomson

Fierce was the wild billow

Fierce was the wild billow,
Dark was the night;
Oars laboured heavily,
Foam glimmered white;
Trembled the mariners,
Peril was nigh:
Then said the God of God,
'Peace! It is I.'

Ridge of the mountain-wave,
Lower thy crest!
Wail of Euroclydon,
Be thou at rest!
Sorrow can never be,
Darkness must fly,
Where saith the Light of Light,
'Peace! It is I.'

Jesus, Deliverer,
Come thou to me;
Soothe thou my voyaging
Over life's sea:
Thou, when the storm of death
Roars, sweeping by,
Whisper, O Truth of Truth,
'Peace! It is I.'

Anatolius (8th century) tr. J M Neale (1818-1866)

A Prayer of Saint Francis of Assisi

Lord, make me an instrument of Thy peace;
where there is hatred, let me sow love;
where there is injury, pardon;
where there is doubt, faith;
where there is despair, hope;
where there is darkness, light;
and where there is sadness, joy.

O Divine Master,
grant that I may not so much seek to be consoled as to console;
to be understood, as to understand;
to be loved, as to love;
for it is in giving that we receive,
it is in pardoning that we are pardoned,
and it is in dying that we are born to Eternal Life.
Amen.

St Francis of Assisi (1182-1226)

Good night

Good-Night. Good-night. Ah, good the night
That wraps thee in its silver light.
Good-night. No night is good for me
That does not hold a thought of thee.
Good-night.

Good-night. Be every night as sweet
As that which made our love complete,
Till that last night when death shall be
One brief 'Good-night' for thee and me.
Good-night.

S Weir Mitchell (1829-1914)

How did you die?

Did you tackle that trouble that came your way
With a resolute heart and cheerful?

Or hide your face from the light of day
With a craven soul and fearful?

Oh, a trouble's a ton, or a trouble's an ounce,
Or a trouble is what you make it.

And it isn't the fact that you're hurt that counts,
But only how did you take it?

You are beaten to earth? Well, well, what's that?
Come up with a smiling face.

It's nothing against you to fall down flat,
But to lie there that's disgrace.

The harder you're thrown, why the higher you bounce;
Be proud of your blackened eye!

It isn't the fact that you're licked that counts;
It's how did you fight and why?

And though you be done to the death, what then ?
If you battled the best you could;

If you played your part in the world of men,
Why, the Critic will call it good.

Death comes with a crawl, or comes with a pounce,
And whether he's slow or spry,

It isn't the fact that you're dead that counts,
But only, how did you die?

Edmund Vance Cooke (1866-1932)

From **The doubter's prayer**

Eternal Power, of earth and air!
Unseen, yet seen in all around;
Remote, but dwelling everywhere;
Though silent heard in every sound;

Then hear me now, while kneeling here,
I lift to Thee my heart and eye,
And all my soul ascends in prayer,
Oh, give me Give me Faith! I cry

What shall I do if all my love,
My hopes, my toil, are cast away,
And if there be no God above,
To hear and bless me while I pray?

If this be vain delusion all,
If death be an eternal sleep
And none can hear my secret call,
Or see the silent tears I weep!

O help me God! for Thou alone
Canst my distracted soul relieve;
Forsake it not, it is Thine own,
Though weak, yet longing to believe.

Anne Bronte (1820-1849)

Faith

I will not doubt, though all my ships at sea
Come drifting home with broken masts and sails;
I shall believe the Hand which never fails,
From seeming evil worketh good to me;
And, though I weep because those sails are battered,
Still will I cry, while my best hopes lie shattered,
'I trust in Thee.'

I will not doubt, though all my prayers return
Unanswered from the still, white realm above;
I shall believe it is an all-wise Love
Which has refused those things for which I yearn;
And though, at times, I cannot keep from grieving,
Yet the pure ardour of my fixed believing
Undimmed shall burn.

I will not doubt, though sorrows fall like rain,
And troubles swarm like bees about a hive;
I shall believe the heights for which I strive,
Are only reached by anguish and by pain;
And, though I groan and tremble with my crosses,
I yet shall see, through my severest losses,
The greater gain.

I will not doubt; well anchored in the faith,
Like some staunch ship, my soul braves every gale,
So strong its courage that it will not fail
To breast the mighty, unknown sea of death.
Oh, may I cry when body parts with spirit,
'I do not doubt,' so listening worlds may hear it
With my last breath.

Ella Wheeler Wilcox (1855-1919)

Who is the angel that cometh?

Who is the Angel that cometh?
Death!
But do not shudder and do not fear;
Hold your breath,
For a kingly presence is drawing near.
Cold and bright
Is his flashing steel,
Cold and bright
The smite that comes like a starry light
To calm the terror and grief we feel;
He comes to help and to save and heal:
Then let us, baring our hearts and kneeling,
Sing, while we wait this Angel's sword,
'Blessed is he that cometh
In the name of the Lord!'

Adelaide Anne Procter 1825-1864

For the fallen

With proud thanksgiving, a mother for her children,
England mourns for her dead across the sea.
Flesh of her flesh they were, spirit of her spirit.
Fallen in the cause of the free.

Solemn the drums thrill: Death august and royal
Sings sorrow up into immortal spheres.
There is music in the midst of desolation
And a glory that shines upon our tears.

They went with songs to the battle, they were young,
Straight of limb, true of eye, steady and aglow.
They were staunch to the end against odds uncounted,
They fell with their faces to the foe.

They shall grow not old, as we that are left grow old:
Age shall not weary them, nor the years condemn.
At the going down of the sun and in the morning
We will remember them.

They mingle not with their laughing comrades again;
They sit no more at familiar tables of home;
They have no lot in our labour of the day-time:
They sleep beyond England's foam.

But where our desires are and our hopes profound,
Felt as a well-spring that is hidden from sight,
To the innermost heart of their own land they are known
As the stars are known to the Night;

As the stars that shall be bright when we are dust
Moving in marches upon the heavenly plain,
As the stars that are starry in the time of our darkness,
To the end, to the end, they remain.

Laurence Binyon (1869-1943)

Death is the way home

God Himself, His thoughts, His will, His love, His judgments are men's home. To think His thoughts, to choose His will, to judge His judgments, and thus to know that He is in us, with us, is to be at home.

And to pass through the valley of the shadow of death is the way home, but only thus, that as all changes have hitherto led us nearer to this home, the knowledge of God, so this greatest of all outward changes — for it is but an outward change — will surely usher us into a region where there will be fresh possibilities of drawing nigh in heart, soul, and mind to the Father of us all.

George Macdonald (1824-1905)

Valley of the shadow

God, I am travelling out to death's sea,
I, who exulted in sunshine and laughter,
Dreamed not of dying — death is such waste of me!
Grant me one prayer: Doom not the hereafter
Of mankind to war, as though I had died not
I, who in battle, my comrade's arm linking,
Shouted and sang, life in my pulses hot
Throbbing and dancing! Let not my sinking
In dark be for naught, my death a vain thing !
God, let me know it the end of man's fever!
Make my last breath a bugle call, carrying
Peace o'er the valleys and cold hills for ever!

John Galsworthy (1867-1933)

Avoid not death

As the production of the metal proveth the work of the alchemist, so is death the test of our lives, the assay which sheweth the standard of all our actions.

He hath not spent his life ill, who knoweth to die well; neither can he have lost all his time, who employeth the last portion of it to his honour. Avoid not death, for it is a weakness; fear it not, for thou understandest not what it is; all that thou certainly knowest is, that it putteth an end to thy sorrows.

Think not the longest life the happiest; that which is best employed, doth man the most honour.

Ancient Indian writer

The two mysteries

We know not what it is, dear, this sleep so deep and still;
The folded hands, the awful calm, the cheek so pale and chill;
The lids that will not lift again, though we may call and call;
The strange white solitude of peace that settles over all.

We know not what it means, dear, this desolate heart pain;
This dread to take our daily way, and walk in it again;
We know not to what other sphere the loved who leave us go,
Nor why we're left to wonder still, nor why we do not know.

But this we know: our loved and dead, if they should come this day,
Should come and ask us, 'What is Life?' not one of us could say.
Life is a mystery, as deep as ever death can be;
Yet, oh, how dear it is to us, this life we live and see!

Then might they say these vanished ones and blessed is the
                                                thought,
'So death is sweet to us, beloved! though we may show you naught;
We may not to the quick reveal the mystery of death
Ye cannot tell us, if ye would, the mystery of breath!'

The child who enters life comes not with knowledge or intent,
So those who enter death must go as little children sent.
Nothing is known. But I believe that God is overhead;
And as life is to the living, so death is to the dead.

Mary Mapes Dodge (1838-1905)

Death

Why be afraid of death, as though your life were breath?
Death but anoints your eyes with clay. O glad surprise !

Why should you be forlorn? Death only husks the corn.
Why should you fear to meet the thresher of the wheat?

Is sleep a thing to dread? Yet sleeping you are dead
Till you awake and rise, here, or beyond the skies.

Why should it be a wrench to leave your wooden bench?
Why not, with happy shout, run home when school is out?

The dear ones left behind? Oh, foolish one and blind!
A day and you will meet a night and you will greet.

This is the death of death, to breathe away a breath
And know the end of strife, and taste the deathless life,

And joy without a fear, and smile without a tear;
And work, nor care to rest, and find the last the best.

Maltbie D Babcock (1858-1901)

When we awake

No man who is fit to live need fear to die. Poor, timorous, faithless souls that we are! How we shall smile at our vain alarms when the worst has happened!

To us here, death is the most terrible thing we know. But when we have tasted its reality, it will mean to us birth, deliverance, a new creation of ourselves. It will be what health is to the sick man. It will be what home is to the exile. It will be what the loved one given back is to the bereaved.

As we draw near to it, a solemn gladness should fill our hearts. It is God's great rooming lighting up the sky. Our fears are the terror of children in the night. The night with its terrors, its darkness, its feverish dreams, is passing away; and when we awake, it will be into the sunlight of God.

George S Merriam (1803-1880)

Mystery

What is this mystery that men call death?
My friend before me lies; in all save breath
He seems the same as yesterday. His face
So like to life, so calm, bears not a trace
Of that great change which all of us so dread.
I gaze on him and say: He is not dead,
But sleeps; and soon he will arise and take
Me by the hand. I know he will awake
And smile on me as he did yesterday;
And he will have some gentle word to say,
Some kindly deed to do; for loving thought
Was warp and woof of which his life was wrought.
He is not dead. Such souls forever live
In boundless measure of the love they give.

Jerome B Bell

From Meditations

How absurd and ridiculous is it, ... as when one doth fall sick and dieth, to take on and wonder as though some strange thing had happened? ...whatsoever is dissolved, it is dissolved into those things, whereof it was compounded.

For every dissolution is either a mere dispersion, of the elements into those elements again whereof everything did consist, or a change, of that which is more solid into earth; and of that which is pure and subtile or spiritual, into air.

So that by this means nothing is lost, but all resumed again into those rational generative seeds of the universe; and this universe, either after a certain period of time to lie consumed by fire, or by continual changes to be renewed, and so for ever to endure.

Marcus Aurelius (121-180 AD)

Make my sleep a holy trance

Make my sleep a holy trance:
That I may, my rest being wrought,
Awake into some holy thought.
And with as active vigour run
My course, as doth the nimble sun.
Sleep is a death, O make me try
By sleeping what it is to die.
And as gently lay my head
On my grave, as now my bed.
Now ere I rest, great God, let me
Awake again at last with Thee.
And thus assured, behold I lie
Securely, or to wake or die.
These are my drowsy days, in vain
I do now wake to sleep again.
O come that hour, when I shall never
Sleep again, but wake for ever!

Thomas Browne (1605-1682)

From **Plato's Apology**

Let us reflect in another way, and we shall see that there is great reason to hope that death is a good, for one of two things:—either death is a state of nothingness and utter unconsciousness, or, as men say, there is a change and migration of the soul from this world to another.

Now if you suppose that there is no consciousness, but a sleep like the sleep of him who is undisturbed even by the sight of dreams, death will be an unspeakable gain.

For if a person were to select the night in which his sleep was undisturbed even by dreams, and were to compare with this the other days and nights of his life, and then were to tell us how many days and nights he had passed in the course of his life better and more pleasantly than this one, I think that any man, I will not say a private man, but even the great king, will not find many such days or nights, when compared with the others.

Now if death is like this, I say that to die is gain; for eternity is then only a single night. But if death is the journey to another place, and there, as men say, all the dead are, what good, O my friends and judges, can be greater than this?

Socrates (c.470- 399BC)

Crossing the bar

Sunset and evening star,
And one clear call for me!
And may there be no moaning of the bar,
When I put out to sea,

But such a tide as moving seems asleep,
Too full for sound and foam,
When that which drew from out the boundless deep
Turns again home.

Twilight and evening bell,
And after that the dark!
And may there be no sadness of farewell,
When I embark;

For tho' from out our bourne of Time and Place
The flood may bear me far,
I hope to see my Pilot face to face
When I have crost the bar.

Alfred, Lord Tennyson (1809-1892)

Death is a friend

I might say much of the commodities that death can sell a man; but briefly, death is a friend of ours, and he that is not ready to entertain him is not at home.

Whilst I am, my ambition is not to move faster than the tide; I have but so to make my interest of it, as I may account for it; I would wish nothing but what might better my days, nor desire any greater place than in the front of good opinion.

I make not love to the continuance of days, but to the goodness of them; nor wish to die, but refer myself to my hour, which the great Dispenser of all things hath appointed me.

Francis Bacon, 1st Viscount St Albans (1561-1626)

The great sun of wisdom

As yonder tower outstretches to the earth
The dark triangle of its shade alone
When the clear day is shining on its top;
So, darkness in the pathway of man's life
Is but the shadow of God's providence,
By the great Sun of wisdom cast thereon;
And what is dark below is light in heaven.

John Greenleaf Whittier (1807-1892)

A Parable of Immortality

I am standing upon the seashore. A ship at my side spreads her white sails to the morning breeze and starts for the blue ocean. She is an object of beauty and strength, and I stand and watch until at last she hangs like a speck of white cloud just where the sea and sky come down to mingle with each other.

Then someone at my side says, 'There she goes!' Gone where?

Gone from my sight...that is all. She is just as large in mast and hull and spar as she was when she left my side and just as able to bear her load of living freight to the place of destination.

Her diminished size is in me, not in her. And just at the moment when someone at my side says, 'There she goes!' there are other eyes watching her coming...and other voices ready to take up the glad shout...'Here she comes!'

Henry Van Dyke (1852-1933)

Death be not proud

Death be not proud, though some have called thee
Mighty and dreadful, for, thou art not so,
For, those, whom thou think'st, thou dost overthrow,
Die not, poor death, nor yet canst thou kill me.

From rest and sleep, which but thy pictures be,
Much pleasure, then from thee, much more must flow,
And soonest our best men with thee doe go,
Rest of their bones, and souls' delivery.

Thou art slave to fate, chance, kings, and desperate men,
And dost with poison, war, and sickness dwell,
And poppy, or charms can make us sleep as well,
And better than thy stroke; why swell'st thou then?

One short sleep past, we wake eternally,
And death shall be no more; death, thou shalt die.

John Donne (1572-1631)

Immanuel subdued death forever

Think of the majesty of that moment in this dying world's history, when Jesus Christ declared that to the Christian death was only a sleep.

Outside of that small dwelling in Capernaum, a great race of men rushed and toiled as they harassed continents and seas; mighty events marshalled themselves into annals and pageants.

What was inside? In one inconspicuous chamber of a now forgotten house, man's Redeemer, unobserved, martyred man's final enemy.

There Immanuel subdued death forever.

Charles S Robinson (1829-1899)

A glorious transfiguration

Whence comes the powerful impression that is made upon us by the tomb? Are a few grains of dust deserving of our veneration? Certainly not; we respect the ashes of our ancestors for this reason only because a secret voice whispers to us that all is not extinguished in them.

It is this that confers a sacred character on the funeral ceremony among all the nations of the globe; all are alike persuaded that the sleep, even of the tomb, is not everlasting, and that death is but a glorious transfiguration.

François-René de Chateaubriand (1768-1848)

From **May I join the choir invisible**

O may I join the choir invisible
Of those immortal dead who live again
In minds made better by their presence: live
In pulses stirr'd to generosity,
In deeds of daring rectitude, in scorn
For miserable aims that end with self,
In thoughts sublime that pierce the night like stars,
And with their mild persistence urge man's search
To vaster issues.
So to live is heaven:
To make undying music in the world,

May I reach
That purest heaven, be to other souls
The cup of strength in some great agony,
Enkindle generous ardor, feed pure love,
Beget the smiles that have no cruelty,
Be the sweet presence of a good diffus'd,
And in diffusion ever more intense!
So shall I join the choir invisible
Whose music is the gladness of the world.

George Eliot (1819-1880)

In the face of eternity

The Christian has virtually ceased nowadays to believe that he will become an angel and spend the timeless space of the everlasting in singing. The wings and the harp and the music are held nowadays to be the childish figments of childlike minds, and the ministers of the gospel have agreed to banish them from their talk of an afterlife out of deference to the fact that humanity has, so to speak, grown up. But those things ought not to be banished; we need them.

In the face of eternity we are as much children to-day as when the world began. We have grown accustomed to the system that governs the universe, we have given commonplace names to things we do not understand, and deceived ourselves, with the names, into the belief that we understand them.

But our vaunted knowledge of the universe is purely a superficial knowledge. We know that the earth revolves on its own axis. Do we know why it revolves? We say that the sun is so many miles from the earth. Do we know any more than Adam knew how it came there, and why it stays immovable in space? We are children in these matters; children who have adopted an air of grown-up wisdom. And because the sun shone through all the yesterdays we call it reasonable to expect that it will shine to-morrow, whereas, in truth, there is no reason in it, but only natural human expectation. Similarly, we dare to 'reason' about death, which, of itself, has never given us any sort of human expectation.

Reason is a useful thing to apply to the commonplace incidents of everyday life, but death is utterly beyond the domain of reason; therefore, we cannot reason about it. We can only have faith, or be lacking in faith, concerning what it conceals. We can speculate concerning its meaning, or we can decide to leave it out of our thoughts, but we cannot argue about it and prove our arguments right before we ourselves die. No. So far as death is concerned, we are still children, and therefore we should do better to cling to childish symbols than to throw them scornfully away.

Wings are suggestive of a state superior to the human state; harps are suggestive of happiness transcending all known forms of human happiness; music is suggestive of an utterly different condition of existence to the conditions of our present existence. In a literal sense they may seem absurd as heirlooms of death, but in a symbolic sense they stand for a higher, finer existence than earthly life; why, then, should we not cling to them?

Far better, surely, to die confident of life to come than to die in despair. And far better than all the arguments in favour of nothingness after death must be the symbols of the wings and the harps and the music, since they serve to uplift mankind rather than to crush mankind down.

Lee Danvers

A Prayer of John Donne

Bring us, O Lord God, at our last awakening into the house and gate of heaven to enter into that gate and dwell in that house, where there shall be no darkness nor dazzling, but one equal light; no noise nor silence, but one equal music; no fears nor hopes, but one equal possession; no ends nor beginnings, but one equal eternity; in the habitations of thy glory and dominion, world without end. Amen.

John Donne (1572-1631)

From **I Am!**

I long for scenes where man hath never trod
A place where woman never smiled or wept
There to abide with my Creator, God,
And sleep as I in childhood sweetly slept,
Untroubling and untroubled where I lie
The grass below—above the vaulted sky.

John Clare (1793-1864)

Also available from Montpelier Publishing:

The Simple Living Companion: Inspiration for a Happier and Less Stressful Life

'I have just three things to teach: simplicity, patience, compassion. These three are your greatest treasures...' (Lao Tzu, Chinese philosopher).

This anthology of quotations and passages on simple living from history's great writers and poets will provide inspiration and motivation on your journey to a simpler, happier life.

Non-Religious Wedding Readings: Poetry and Prose for Civil Marriage Ceremonies

Civil marriage ceremonies are increasingly popular, but it can be difficult to choose readings which are appropriate in a non-religious setting. A few well-known poems tend to appear regularly at civil ceremonies, but if you are looking for something different, this book could be the answer.

Non-Religious Funeral Readings: Philosophy and Poetry for Secular Services

In recent years non-religious funerals have become more common, but without an established canon of readings to fall back on, it can be difficult to plan an appropriate service for a loved one who had no religious belief or connections.

This book, however, provides opening sentences, readings, and sentences for committal and/or dispersal from some of the greatest philosophers and writers in history including Marcus Aurelius, Plato, Christina Rossetti, Shakespeare and Rabindranath Tagore.

They retain the solemnity, grandeur and dignity of the traditional language of Christian funerals found in the King James Bible and the Book of Common Prayer, but make no dogmatic references to religion, the supernatural or life after death; beliefs which many today do not or cannot hold. Instead, the readings offer a positive philosophical approach to death, and a celebration of the life and memory of the departed.